LET'S GO OUTSIDE!

DOVER PUBLICATIONS, INC.
MINEOLA, NEW YORK

education.com

Bibliographical Note

Let's Go Outside!, first published by Dover Publications, Inc., in 2015, contains pages from the following online workbooks published by Education.com: *All About Animals, Explore the Outdoors, Plant Parts,* and *Weather Watchers.*

International Standard Book Number

ISBN-13: 978-0-486-80259-6
ISBN-10: 0-486-80259-0

Manufactured in the United States by Courier Corporation
80259001   2015
www.doverpublications.com

CONTENTS

All About Animals 1

Explore the Outdoors 33

Plant Parts 67

Weather Watchers 97

Answers 121

ALL ABOUT ANIMALS

Living or Non-Living?

Look at the pictures below. Which ones are examples of living things and which ones are not? Place a green circle around all of the pictures of living things. Draw a red X over all of the non-living things.

Where Do Animals Make Their Homes?

All living things need a place to live. Look at each animal below and decide where it might live. Draw a line to match the animal to its correct shelter or home.

bear

child

squirrel

fish

Now fill in the blank spaces below to make the sentences complete.
Use the words and pictures above for clues.

1. A bear lives in a _____.

2. A _____ lives in a house.

3. A squirrel lives in a _____.

4. A fish lives in a _____.

Living things	Non-Living things

Living / Non-Living Mix-Up

Look at these pictures. Some are examples of living things, and others are examples of non-living things.

Cut out each picture below and sort them by living and non-living. Then glue your pictures onto the correct side of the T-chart on the previous page.

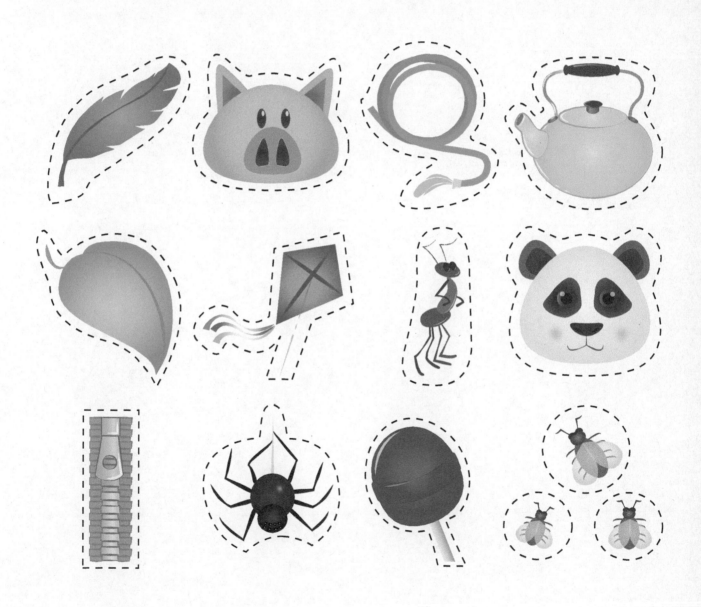

Hunting For Animal Homes

Animals need shelter in order to survive, and there are many different types of animal homes! Can you find these different shelters in the word puzzle below?

HINT: *Make sure you look backwards and diagonally.*

Word Bank:

house	underground	tunnel	tree	pond	ocean	forest
cave	nest	hive	den	burrow	web	barn
kennel	stable	coop	sty			

```
H L E N P X W P O N D B K E Z
F P S A L Z J N U N X Z S E W
Y Q I E B Q Y Q U N B N S T Y
H U R C C B B O H F Q E G N H
H Y Y O E X R C C Q M D O U E
H Z X W Q G T P A O P M P B U
B T F R R N G N Q V I W S N D
S I T E H G B W E T E J L E K
I L D I E L B A T S W H K S H
A N V I F A U H T D U E R T B
U E I X Z O R R L H N O G B W
T U N N E L R E X N P E H Z I
J E A W Z V O E E X E O E Q J
N R A B A S W L S R N N O L F
Y S V N X C T P T T H Q M C R
```

7

Hunting For Home

Can you help these animals safely find their way home? Each animal takes a different path in the maze below. Use a different color to trace each animal's path back home to its habitat.

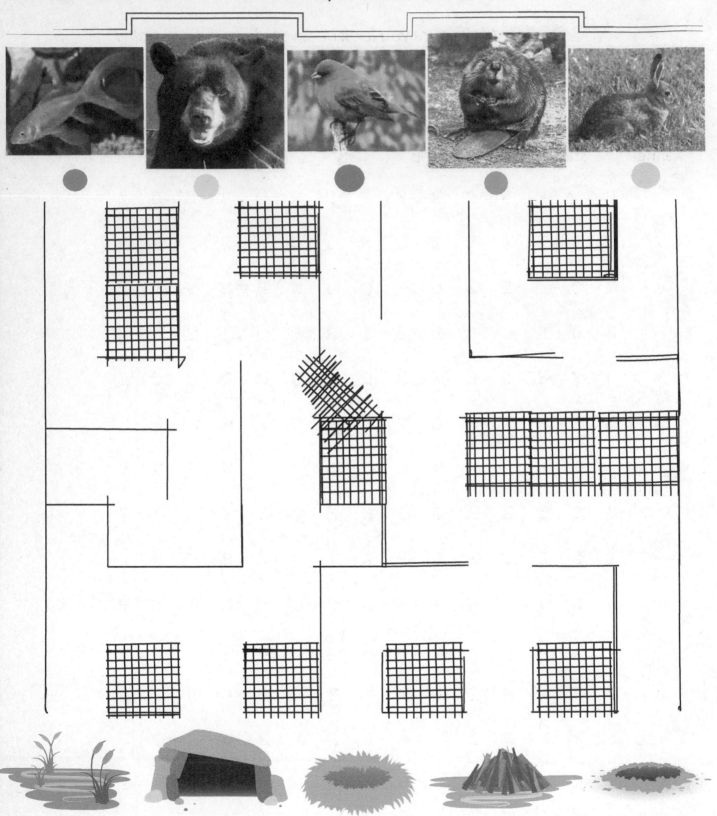

ANIMALS BUILDING HOMES

Read the paragraph below about animals building their homes. Then answer the reading comprehension questions at the bottom of the page.

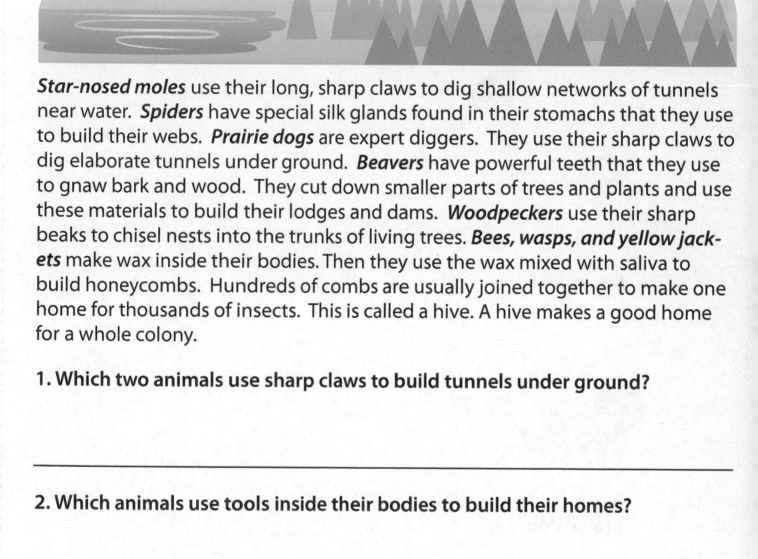

Star-nosed moles use their long, sharp claws to dig shallow networks of tunnels near water. **Spiders** have special silk glands found in their stomachs that they use to build their webs. **Prairie dogs** are expert diggers. They use their sharp claws to dig elaborate tunnels under ground. **Beavers** have powerful teeth that they use to gnaw bark and wood. They cut down smaller parts of trees and plants and use these materials to build their lodges and dams. **Woodpeckers** use their sharp beaks to chisel nests into the trunks of living trees. **Bees, wasps, and yellow jackets** make wax inside their bodies. Then they use the wax mixed with saliva to build honeycombs. Hundreds of combs are usually joined together to make one home for thousands of insects. This is called a hive. A hive makes a good home for a whole colony.

1. Which two animals use sharp claws to build tunnels under ground?

_____

2. Which animals use tools inside their bodies to build their homes?

_____

3. Which two animals use trees to build their homes? Explain how.

_____

CAN YOU BUILD THESE ANIMAL HOMES?

Now that you have learned about HOW some animals build their homes, can you help to show WHAT each shelter would look like? Look at each animal picture below. In the box next to each animal, draw a picture to show what its home or shelter would look like!

woodpecker

honey bee

prairie dog

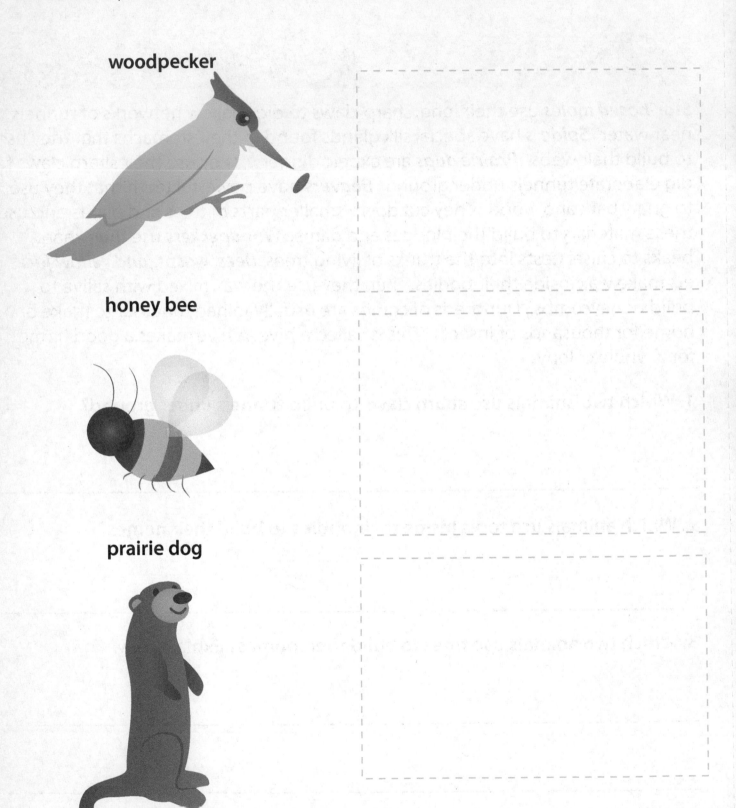

CAN YOU BUILD THESE ANIMAL HOMES?

spider

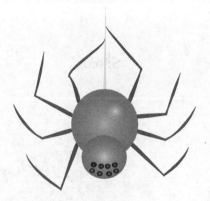

beaver

star-nosed mole

What'S foR dinneR?

All living things need food and water in order to survive!
Look at each animal below. What might these animals eat in order to survive and thrive? Draw your ideas inside the boxes.

squirrel

snake

horse

shark

butterfly

lion

puppy

frog

What, Oh What Should I Wear?

Different animals wear different types of body coverings. Can you place each animal below in the correct category? Give it a try!

Directions: Cut apart the animal pictures at the bottom of the page. Then paste them into the correct category on the animal coverings diagram.

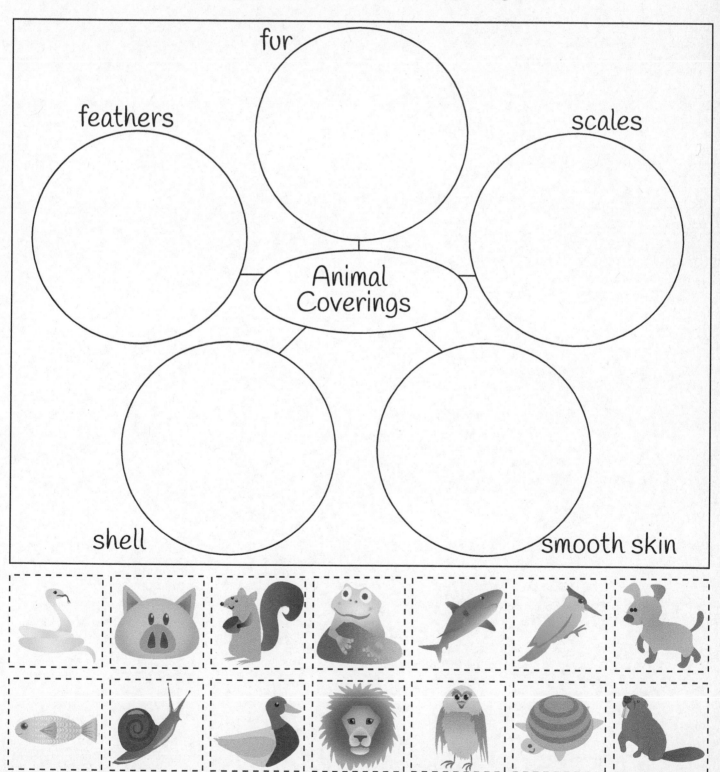

Animal Coverings

Animals have different features that help them to survive in different places. These features (also called body coverings) include fur or hair, shells, scales, skin, and feathers.

Can you find the correct body covering for each animal below?

If the animal is covered with **fur**, color it **orange**.

If the animal is covered by **scales**, color it **green**.

If the animal has **feathers**, color it **blue**.

If the animal has **skin**, color it **pink**.

fish

beaver

bird

frog

pig

skunk

bat

cow

snake

lizard

Animal Coverings:
Memory Match-Up Game!

Animals have different features that help them to survive in different places. These features (also called body coverings) include fur or hair, shells, scales, skin, and feathers.

Can you match the animals with their correct body coverings? Here's a game to test your skills!

Game Rules and Set-Up

1. Cut apart the animal cards on the next page using the dotted lines as a guide.
2. Then cut apart the body covering cards on page 19 in the same way.
3. Mix all of your cards together and place them in one large pile.
4. Now build a memory board lining your cards up to make a big square (4 cards across and 6 cards down).
5. Each player turns over two different cards at the same time. If they match (tiger/fur or snake/scales) then you get to keep the cards! If they don't match, then you must flip them back over in their place on the board and it is the next player's turn.
6. The game continues until all matches have been found and there are no more cards left on your memory board! The player who has the most matches in the end is the winner!

Animal Coverings:
Memory Match-Up Game!

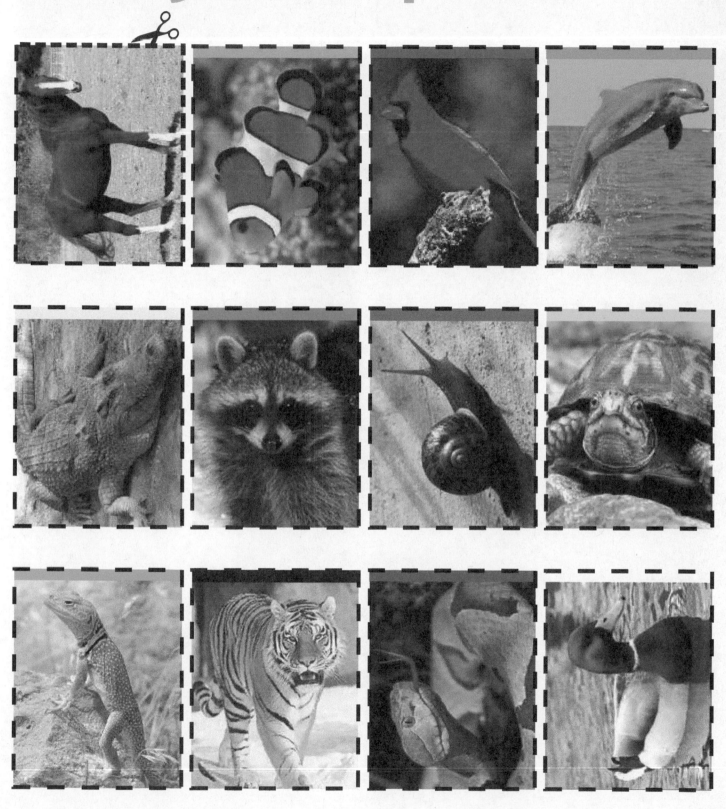

Animal Coverings:
Memory Match-Up Game!

Animal Camouflage

Some animals have body coverings that help them to blend in with their habitat. This is called **camouflage.**
Draw a line to connect each animal with the camouflage habitat that it belongs to.

In the spaces below, write down the key color that each animal relies on to camouflage itself in its habitat.

_____ _____ _____ _____ _____

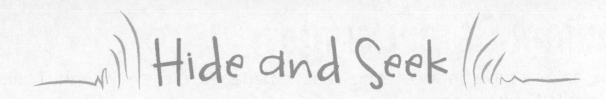

Hide and Seek

Many animals must blend into their surroundings in order to hide from their enemies. The colors or patterns that an animal has can help it hide from dangerous predators and stay safe in its own habitat.

Directions: Color the animals on pages 23–29 to make sure each creature stays safe in its habitat.

Remember that each animal's coloring and body patterns will need to blend into its surroundings in order to be protected!

Use lots of COLOR and detail to make each animal look like it would in its natural habitat.

HINT: Think about the scenery you will need to add in order to keep each animal safe!

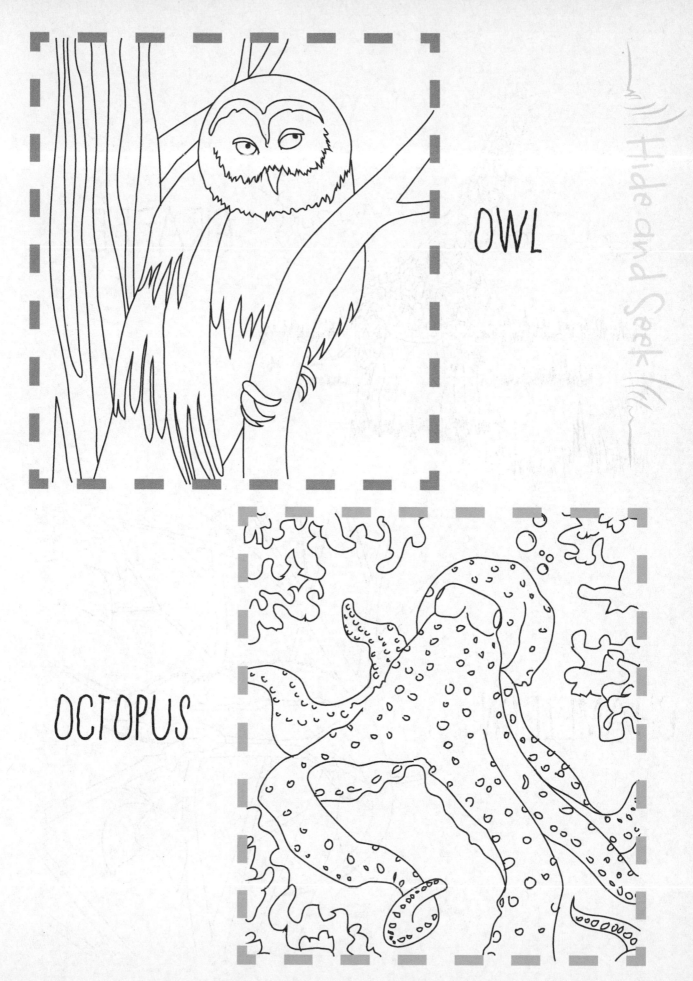

OWL

OCTOPUS

GIRAFFE

CHAMELEON

Hide and Seek

24

TIGER

COBRA

CROCODILE

MOOSE

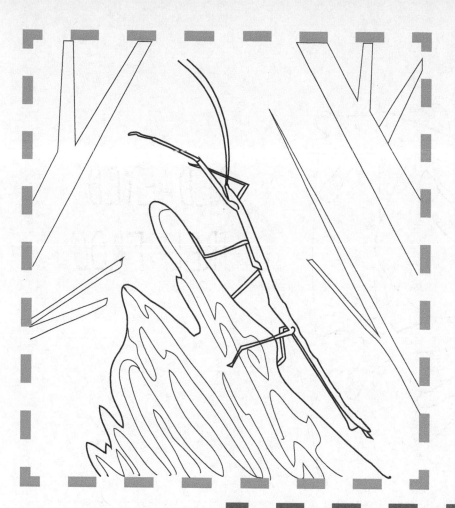

WALKING
STICK

TOUCAN

27

RED-EYED
TREE FROG

LION

RABBIT

BEAVER

MY HOME

Draw a picture of your home!

What are a few words that describe your home?

_____

Write a sentence about your favorite part of your house:

_____

_____

Great job!

_____

is an Education.com science superstar

EXPLORE THE OUTDOORS

LET'S EXPLORE
THE
OUTDOORS

THIS NATURE JOURNAL BELONGS TO:

_____

MY GOALS FOR THE OUTDOORS

A GOAL IS SOMETHING YOU WANT TO DO OR ACHIEVE. IT IS IMPORTANT TO SET GOALS AS A WAY TO CHALLENGE YOURSELF, AND IT IS A GREAT FEELING WHEN YOU MEET YOUR GOALS. USE THE SPACE BELOW TO WRITE SOME GOALS FOR YOUR OUTDOOR EXPLORATION!

☐ I WANT TO VISIT _____ NATIONAL PARK.

☐ I WANT TO SEE _____

☐ I WANT TO RUN/WALK ___ MILES IN ___ MONTHS.

☐ EVERY WEEK I WILL PLAY _____ OUTSIDE.

☐ EVERY DAY I WILL GO _____ OUTSIDE.

☐ I WANT TO LEARN HOW TO _____

☐ I WANT TO HIKE AT _____

☐ I WANT TO CAMP AT _____

☐ I WANT TO _____

☐ I WANT TO _____

Magnifying Glass

A magnifying glass is a tool we use to help us see things that are very, very small. This is an important item for all outdoor explorers to have! Draw some of the things you've looked at with your magnifying glass.

Animal Tracks Checklist

While walking through the woods, look out for signs that animals have been there before you.
Check the soft ground like sand, mud, or snow, for animal tracks. Mammals of the dog and cat families walk on four toes. You can see the claws in dog's prints, but cats retract their claws. Bears, raccoons, and rodents walk on five toes. Some animals have human-like hands, and others have hooves.
The animals pictured below are all **North American Animals.**

When you go on hikes, carry this checklist and check off the animal tracks you see.

☐ Bear

☐ Deer

☐ Raccoon

☐ Fox

☐ Badger

☐ Porcupine

☐ Coyote

☐ Bobcat

☐ Opossum

☐ Wild Turkey

☐ Wolf

☐ Squirrel

Bug Identification Chart

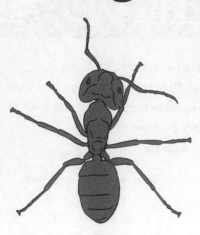

Ant
Ant colonies have one queen who lays thousands of eggs.

Bee
Bees help plants grow by spreading the pollen around to other plants.

Spider
Some spiders build web communities where up to 50,000 spiders may live.

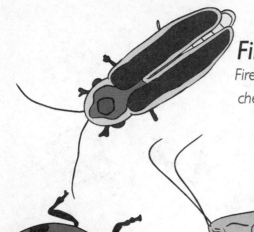

Firefly
Fireflies produce light with chemicals in their bodies.

Ladybug
Ladybugs protect crops by eating plant-eating insects like aphids.

Grasshopper
An adult grasshopper can leap 10 times its length.

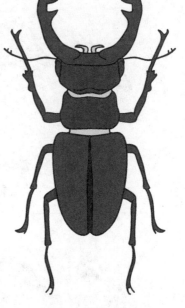

Stag Beetle
The large antlers on a stag beetle are really mandibles, which are its jaws.

Now it's time to go outdoors for some observation. That means watching and noticing important or interesting things about an object. Find 4 insects that you like and draw them in the spaces below. Then write down 1 or 2 observations about each insect!

Color: _____ Shape: _____

This insect is: _____

Color: _____ Shape: _____

This insect is: _____

Color: _____ Shape: _____

This insect is: _____

Color: _____ Shape: _____

This insect is: _____

Flower Identification Chart

Poppy

This is the state flower of California.

Bluebell

This purple flower hangs like a bell.

Dandelion

This flower's name means lion's tooth.

Daisy

Daisy means "day's eye" because daisies open as soon as the day begins.

Sunflower

The sunflower's bloom looks like the sun.

Honeysuckle

Many honeysuckles have a sweet smell. They are bell shaped and make a nectar that you can eat.

40

Now it's time to go outdoors for some observation. That means watching and noticing important or interesting things about an object. Find 4 flowers that you like and draw them in the spaces below. Then write down 1 or 2 observations about each flower!

Color: _ _ _ _ Shape: _ _ _ _

This flower is: _ _ _ _

Color: _ _ _ _ Shape: _ _ _ _

This flower is: _ _ _ _

Color: _ _ _ _ Shape: _ _ _ _

This flower is: _ _ _ _

Color: _ _ _ _ Shape: _ _ _ _

This flower is: _ _ _ _

Name the different parts of a plant

Choose the correct word from the bottom of the page to name each part of the plant.

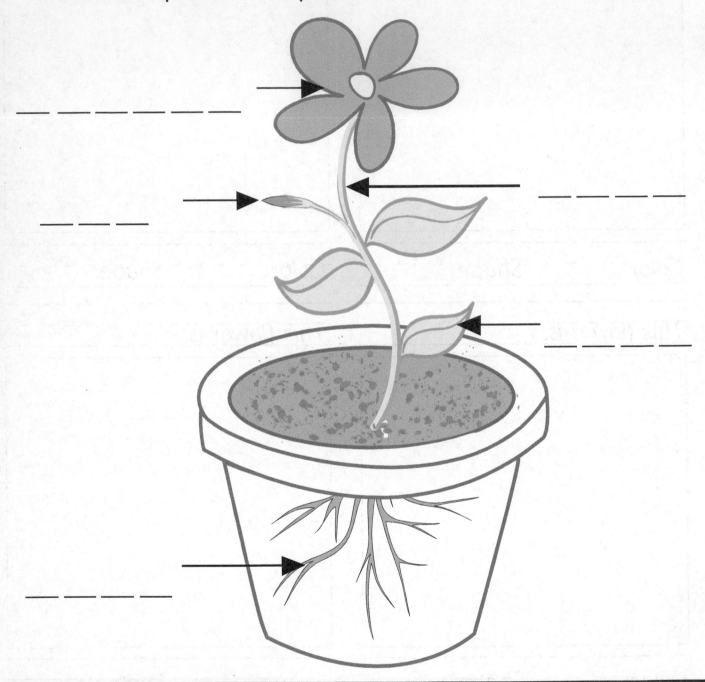

_ _ _ _ _ _ _

_ _ _ _

_ _ _ _ _ _

_ _ _ _ _

_ _ _ _

stem   flower   root   bud   leaf

WHAT IS PHOTOSYNTHESIS

Look at the picture and fill in the blanks using the words at the bottom of the page.

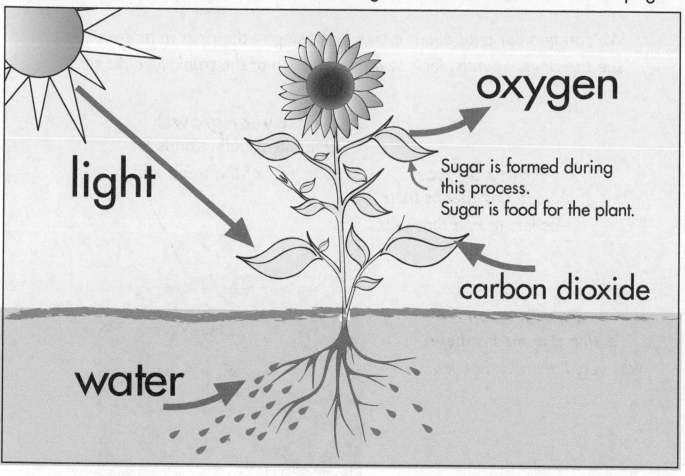

Photosynthesis is a process where plants use _____ from the sun to convert _____ from the air and _____ from the soil into _____ to feed the plant and _____ is given out in the air.

water,   sugar,   carbon dioxide,   light,   oxygen

Tree Rings

We can find out a lot about a tree by looking at the rings in its trunk. To see the rings, we must look at a cross section of the trunk, just like this!

First year growth
One ring usually stands for one year of the tree's life.

Rainy Season
A wide ring means there was lots of rain that year.

Dry Season
A thin ring means there was very little rain that year.

Fire Damage
A dark mark means the tree was damaged that year.

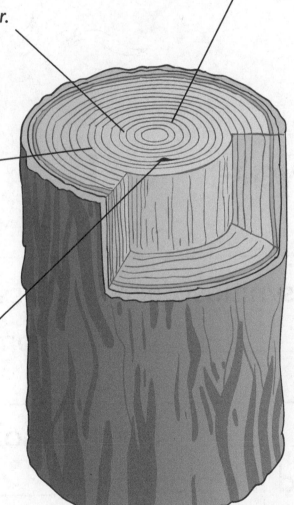

Activity

On your next outdoor adventure, if you come across a tree stump, take a look at its rings. Can you count how old the tree was? Did it have any damage?
Draw a picture of it here:

Yellowstone National Park,
Wyoming, Montana, and Idaho
Yellowstone was the very first national park.
It's so big it is part of three different states!

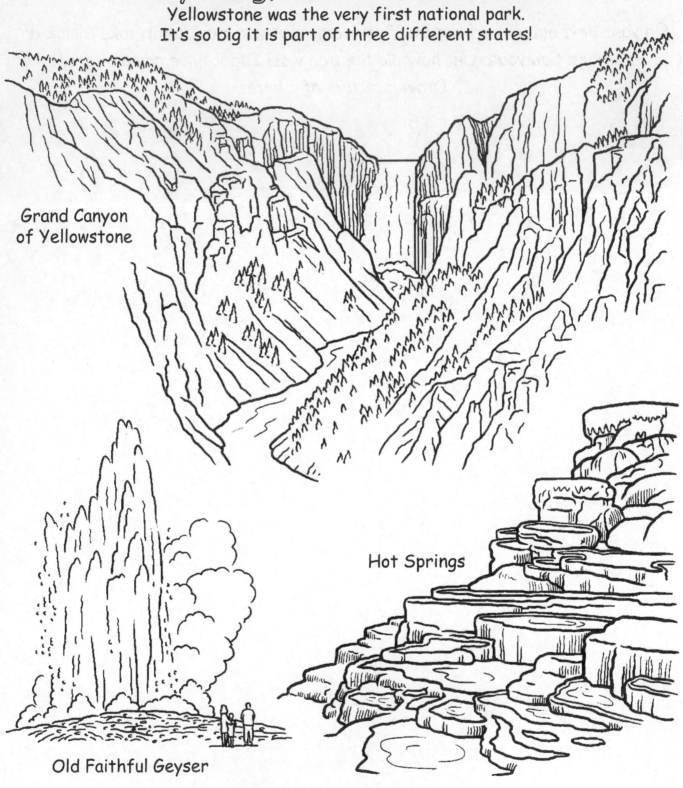

Grand Canyon
of Yellowstone

Hot Springs

Old Faithful Geyser

Grand Canyon, Arizona

The Grand Canyon was created over the course of two billion years. It is considered to be one of the wonders of the natural world!

National Parks

National parks are large areas of protected land. It is important for the United States to keep these parks safe so they can be enjoyed by everyone for a long time. There are over 400 protected areas in the U.S., and 59 of these protected areas are officially known as national parks.

Petrified Forest, Arizona

Grand Canyon, Arizona

Many places are protected because they are a special part of nature.

Other national parks exist to protect endangered animals living there.

Everglades, Florida

Biscayne, Florida

Other places are protected because they are an important part of our country's history.

Great Sand Dunes, Colorado

Mesa Verde, Colorado

Did You know...

The first national park was Yellowstone, in Wyoming, established in 1872.

The newest national park is the Pinnacles National Park, established in 2013.

The pools in Hot Springs National Park are known to have healing powers.

The wood in the Petrified Forest National Park is 225 million years old.

Redwoods in Redwood National Park are the tallest species of tree.

There are rocks in the Grand Canyon that are 2 billion years old.

The lava in the Hawaii Volcanoes is 2,150 degrees.

Activity

Do you know any of the National Parks in your state? List the ones you know, and explain why each park is a special part of nature or U.S. history.

National Parks Map

The United States has 59 National Parks. Here are some of the most famous parks. If you can think of any National Parks that are missing on this map, fill them in!

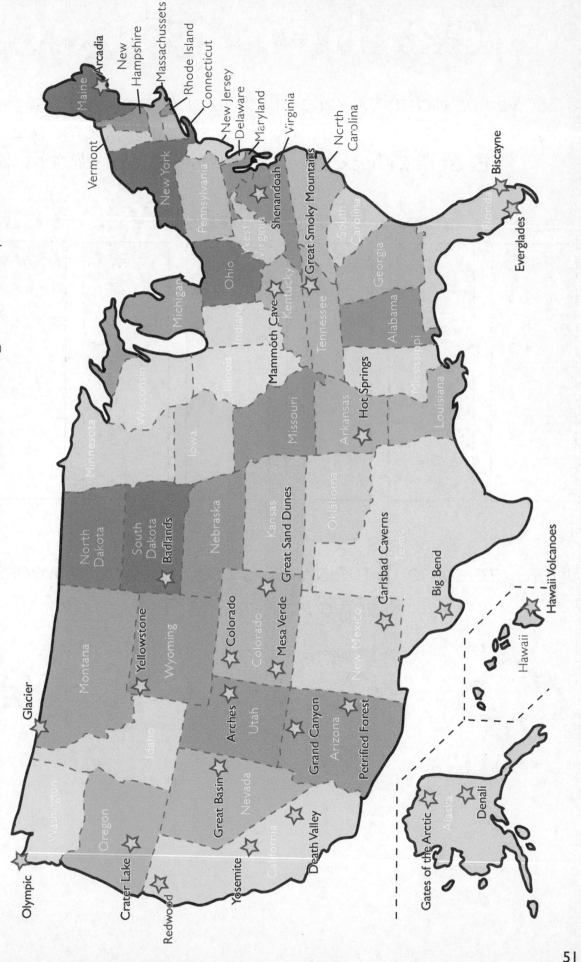

Weather Forecast

Can you predict the weather? Draw a picture of what the weather looks like today, and how you think the weather will look the rest of the week. Each day, check to see how close your predictions were!

Sat	Sun	Mon	Tue	Wed	Thur	Fri

Here are some of the symbols used to write a weather forecast. Can you guess what they mean?

LABEL THE CLOUDS

DIRECTIONS: Label the types of clouds based on the definitions below

CIRRUS — High-altitude feathery thin, white, curly shaped clouds.
CIRROCUMULUS — High-altitude, small, wispy, patchy, puffy, clouds that form in rows.
CIRROSTRATUS — High-altitude thin whispy clouds. When they cover the sky, they are so thin that it looks like a white sheet.
CUMULUS — Low-altitude fluffy white clouds, typical of hot weather.
STRATUS — Low-altitude horizontal, grey, wispy clouds.
NIMBOSTRATUS — Low-altitude dark rain clouds.

SHADOWS

Hi everyone! My name is Dill — short for Can Dill. I'm here to teach you about shadows.

A shadow is created when an object blocks light. All solid objects have a shadow. Take a look at my friend here. The shadow on the ground is created by the light of my flame being blocked by the mouse's shape.

When you're outside the sun casts shadows everywhere. Shadows appear in different positions based on the time of day.

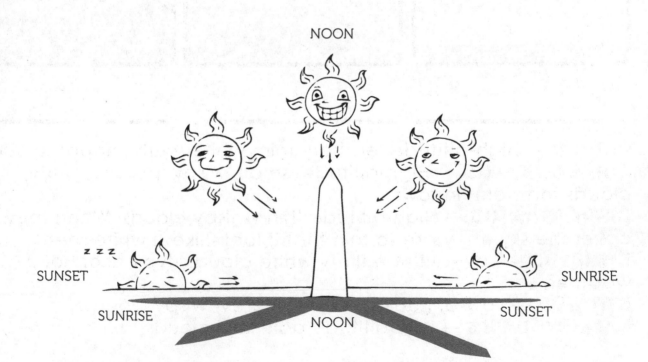

On a sunny day, place an object outdoors, Check on it every two hours. Has the shadow moved? Each time you check on it, draw a picture of the object and its shadow in the boxes below.

Make sure to draw the object from the same position!

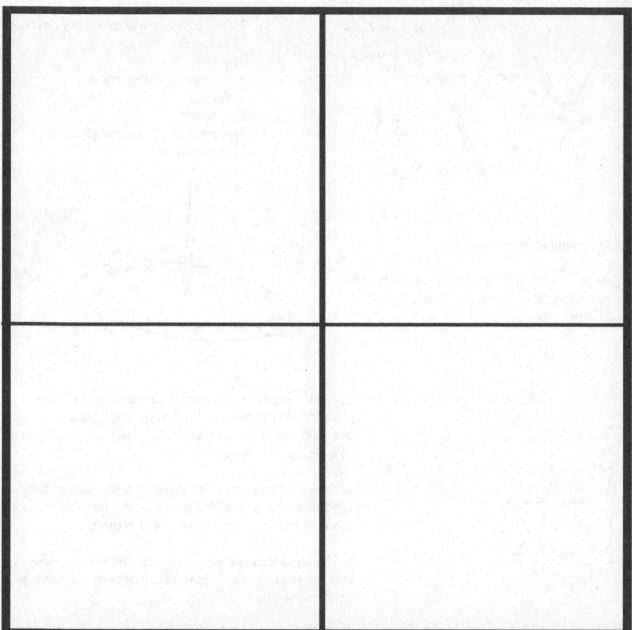

Where do you think the shadow will be tomorrow at 10 a.m.?

_____

Make Your Own Sundial

Remember: Never look directly at the sun.

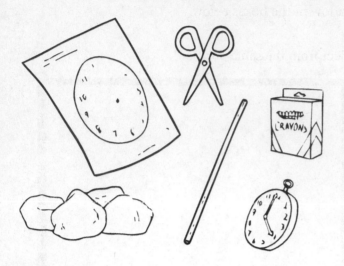

What You Need:

1) The sundial template on the next page
2) Scissors
3) 4 rocks
4) A straw or coffee stirrer
5) A clock
6) Crayons
7) A piece of cardboard (optional)
8) Pieces of tape

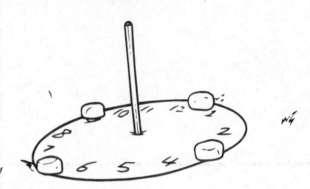

1) Cut out the sundial on the next page.

2) Decorate your sundial, filling in the circle with numbers so that it looks like a clock. Feel free to use more than just crayons to decorate it!

3) Take everything outside and put your sundial on the ground. Use the rocks to hold down the sundial and stop the wind from blowing it away. You maybe want to glue it to a piece of cardboard.

4) Stick the straw or coffee stirrer in the center of the sundial, so that it goes into the ground if possible. You can use tape here to secure the straw into place.

5. Use a clock to see what time it is. Turn your sundial so that the shadow cast by the straw points to the correct hour on the dial.

6) Observe how the shadow moves like the hands on a clock. Why does the shadow move?

Sundial

If you need help cutting, ask a grown-up for help.

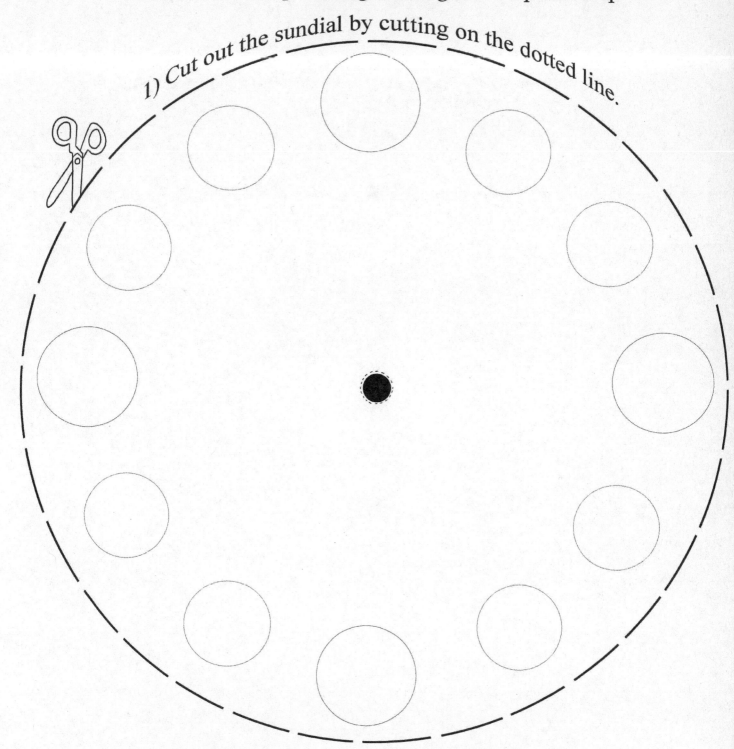

1) Cut out the sundial by cutting on the dotted line.

2) Cut out the small black hole in the center of the sundial.
3) Use your crayons to fill in the 12 other circles with numbers like on a clock.
4) Decorate your sundial! Have fun and use your favorite colors!

Ursa Major (big bear)

A woman named Callisto was turned into a bear by the angry goddess, Hera, and was put up in the sky, where she still lives today. The orange stars are known as the Big Dipper.

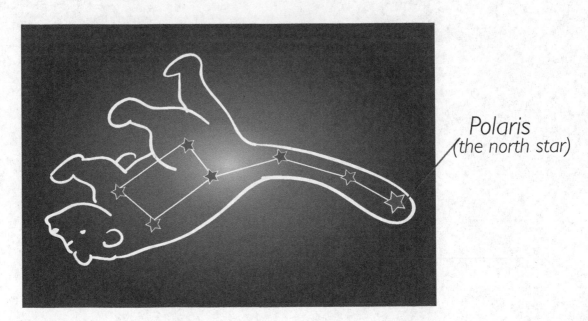

Polaris (the north star)

Ursa Minor (little bear)

The little bear is Arcas, Callisto's son. He was also turned into a bear and put up in the sky. The orange stars are known as the little Dipper.
Polaris (the north star) is the tail of the little dipper, an important star that hunters and travelers can use as a compass to find north.

Orion

Orion was a hunter in ancient Greek mythology. After he was killed by a scorpion, the gods put him up in the sky. Orion's Belt is made up of the three brightest stars in the Orion constellation.

Sirius (the dog star)

Orion's hunting dog Sirius is the brightest star in the sky!

Cassiopeia

Cassiopeia was a very vain, self-centered queen. The gods hung her upside-down in the sky as punishment.

Cepheus

Cepheus, the king, was Cassiopeia's husband.

Lyra/Lyre

The lyra was a stringed instrument that Orpheus used to charm wild animals. When he died, the lyra was placed in the sky to honor him.

Aquila

Aquila was an eagle of the gods. He did many things for the gods, such as carry Zeus' thunderbolts.

Great job!

_____

is an Education.com science superstar

PLANT PARTS

What does a Plant Need?

People need water, food, and air to live. Plants also need certain things to live. We need part of the air called oxygen (O_2). Plants use another part of the air called carbon dioxide (CO_2). Plants take in minerals and food from the soil. Plants need carbon dioxide, water, and sunlight to live. When the plant breathes, it changes the carbon dioxide into oxygen.

Draw a **line** to all the things a plant needs to grow healthy.
Circle the type of air plants breath out.

What Do Plants Need?

Circle all the things plants need to grow.

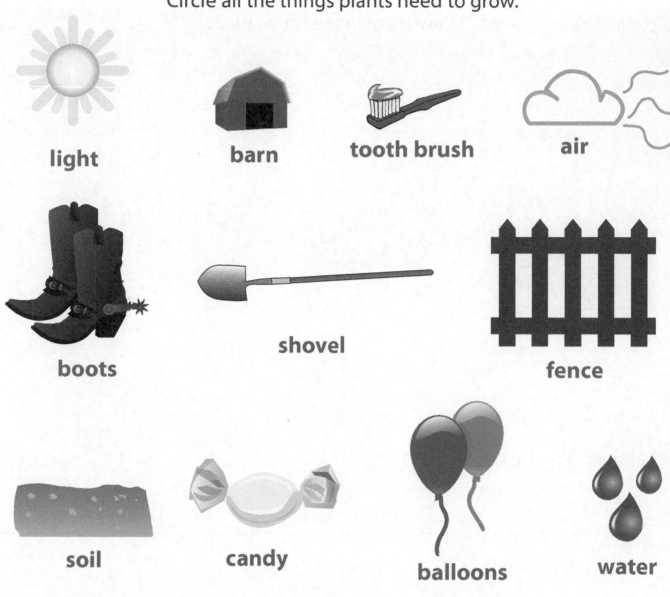

light

barn

tooth brush

air

boots

shovel

fence

soil

candy

balloons

water

How many items did you circle? _____

Why are these items important for all plants?

_____

_____

What Affects Plant Growth?

What are the 4 main things that all plants need to grow?
Draw them in the boxes below.

What happens when plants get too much sun?

_____

What happens when plants don't get enough water?

_____

What things can cause a plant to not grow at all?

_____

Parts of a Plant

Unscramble the letters to name the different parts of a plant. Then draw your own plant to go with your labels and color your picture.

ubd

_ _ _

rolwef

_ _ _ _ _ _

tmse

_ _ _ _

elaf

_ _ _ _

otor

_ _ _ _

Parts of a Plant

Stem

The stem supports the plant so that it stands upright. It has many thin tubes that carry water, minerals, and food up from the roots.

Chlorophyll

This chemical is the green color found in plants. Chlorophyll takes in light from the sun and turns it into energy and sugar to feed the plant. This process is called *photosynthesis*.

Flower

The flower of a plant has many parts. Some flowers make fruit. Others are poisonous to eat. All flowers make *pollen*. The pollen is released into the wind or gets stuck on insects, and when the pollen reaches other flowers, new flowers are made. This process is called *pollination*.

Roots

The roots of a plant are usually underground. Roots soak up water, vitamins and minerals from the soil so that a plant has plenty of food and nutrients. Roots also help to anchor the plant in the soil so that it does not fall over.

Cells

A plant cell is the smallest part of the plant. Plant cells are like animal cells but they have a cell wall and contain *chlorophyll*, which gives the different parts of a plant their green color.

Leaves

Most of the plant's food is made in its leaves. They are wide so that the *chlorophyll* can take in more sunlight and do its job better.

How well do you know your plant parts? Answer the questions below by circling the correct answer under each sentence. Refer to the *Parts of a Plant Vocabulary* worksheet to study for this quiz.

1. What part of a plant makes the most food?

    A. stem   B. fruit   C. flower   D. leaf

2. Which part of a fower is released into the air?

    A. stem   B. root   C. petals   D. pollen

3. Which part of a plant helps keep the plant in an upright position?

    A. stem   B. root   C. sun   D. branch

4. What makes the color of plant leaves green?

    A. chlorophyll   B. green paint   C. oxygen   D. cells

5. Which of the following is the smallest part of a plant?

    A. plant seed   B. plant cell   C. flower   D. leaf

6. Which part of a plant collects water and nutrients from the soil?

    A. stem   B. fruit   C. flower   D. leaf

A seed is like an egg. It is where a baby plant starts its life. Seeds are found in flowers and fruit. They come in many shapes and sizes. When a fruit falls to the ground, its seeds drop into the soil. Rain helps by pushing the seeds all the way into the soil. Once a seed is in the soil, the baby plant will burst out of its outer seed coat and begin to grow!

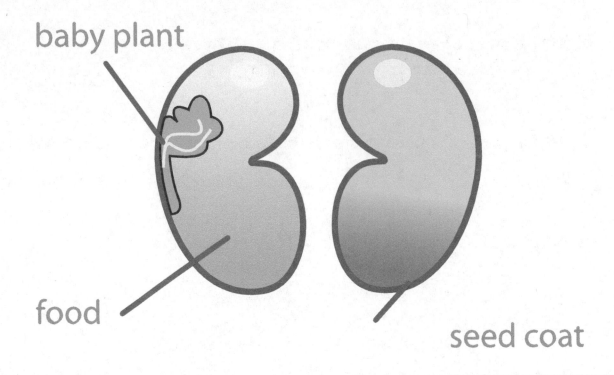

baby plant

food

seed coat

Plants grow from seeds. Inside each seed is an *embryo*, or baby plant. The embryo is surrounded by a food storage area. All seeds have a protective outer layer called the *seed coat*, just like an eggshell! Once the baby seed grows out of its coat, it's called a *seedling*. Then the baby seed grows roots to get minerals and water from the soil. As its stems grow, it also sprouts leaves, which will allow it to make its own food from sunlight. The adult plant will grow flowers and fruits to spread more seeds and start the plant life cycle again.

Ready to test your knowledge? Go to the next page for a short quiz.

Use page 74 to answer the questions. Circle **all** correct answers.

1. Where do plant seeds come from?

a. stem   b. leaves   c. fruit   d. flowers   e. roots

2. What is another name for the baby plant inside the seed?

a. seed coat   b. embryo   c. food storage

3. What is the name of the protective layer of the seed?

a. stem   b. leaves   c. seed coat   d. food storage

4. What do the seed's roots absorb from the soil?

a. water   b. minerals   c. sun rays   d. dirt

5. What is a baby plant called when it grows out of its coat?

a. plant   b. baby seed   c. seedling   d. stem

6. What do the leaves of the plant make?

a. water   b. air   c. food   d. sunlight

7. What do adult plants grow to continue the plant life cycle?

a. stem   b. leaves   c. flowers   d. fruit

8. What is a seed most like?

a. an egg   b. a baby   c. a tree   d. an apple

How Do Seeds Get Planted By Nature?

drop

Some seeds drop out of the flower onto the ground.

wind

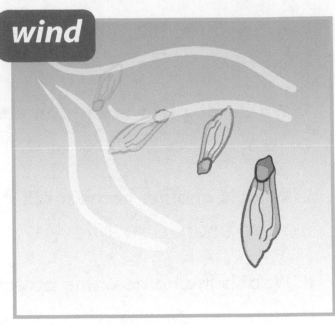

Some seeds travel by wind.

water

Some seeds float in the water to get to land.

animals

Some seeds spread when they are carried by animals or bugs.

1. What is a type of seed that travels to land by water?

_____

2. How do animals help plant seeds?

_____

_____

3. How can seeds travel by air?

_____

_____

4. What is another way seeds are planted by nature?

_____

_____

Did you know...
Maple seeds have wings so they can travel by air.

Seeds, Fruit, and Plants

Draw a line to match each food item with the correct plant or tree it comes from.

Did you know that we eat many different parts of the plant? We eat the **stem** of the plant when we eat asparagus or celery. We eat the **leaves** of the plant when we eat lettuce. We eat the yummy **fruits** of the plant, and those fruits have seeds inside of them. Sometimes we can eat the seeds, like when we eat strawberries or cucumbers, and sometimes we don't like to eat the seeds, like when we eat apples or grapes. When we eat veggies like corn or peas, we are actually eating the **seeds** from the plant! When we eat other veggies like carrots or potatoes, we are eating the **roots** of the plant. Cauliflower, artichoke, and broccoli plants produce **flowers** that are tasty to eat.

Sometimes we eat more than one part of the plant. Many people like the root of the beet plant, but the leaves are also yummy. Beet leaves are used in salads when the leaves are young and tender. When they get bigger, beet leaves can be bitter, so they taste better cooked. We usually eat the root of the onion plant, but the stems taste good too, when they are young and tender.

Some of the plants we eat are *poisonous* if we eat the wrong part. Did you know that the leaves of a tomato plant are poisonous? For many years people would not even eat tomatoes because they thought the entire plant was poisonous! Now we know the fruit of the tomato plant is safe and delicious, plus it has vitamins that are very good for us too!

Now think about the plant facts you just read above. On the next page, answer the questions. You may look back at the facts for help.

We Eat!

1. Which part of a plant can we eat? *(Circle **all** correct answers.)*

a. stem   b. leaves   c. fruit   d. seeds   e. flowers

2. We eat more than one part of these plants: *(Circle **one** answer.)*

a. spinach and lettuce   b. okra and tomatoes
c. beets and onions   d. radish and carrot

3. When are beet leaves good to eat?

_____ .

4. The fruit of this plant is delicious, but the leaves are poisonous.

It is a _____ .

5. What is a plant that you love to eat?_____

What type of plant part is it?   *(Circle **all** answers that apply.)*

a. stem   b. leaves   c. fruit
d. seeds   e. flowers

Now match the plants to the parts we eat!

roots

stems

leaves

seeds

flowers

PLANT LIFE CYCLE

HOW DO PLANTS GROW ?

Paste the flash cards you cut out from the next page in these boxes in the correct sequence.

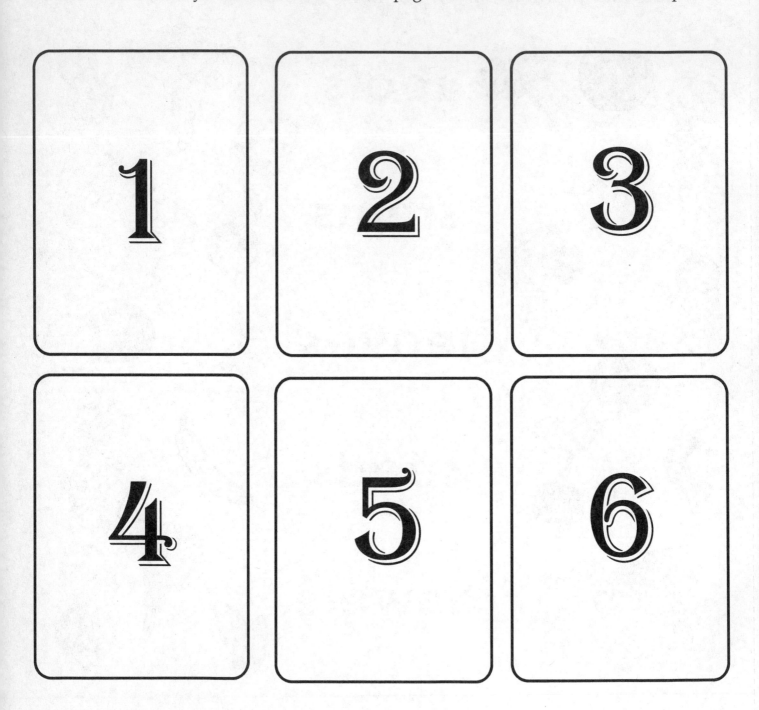

PLANT LIFE CYCLE

HOW DO PLANTS GROW?

Cut out the flash cards with the help of a grown-up. Then paste the cards in the correct sequence on the previous page.

SPROUT

WATER

SOIL

SUNLIGHT

PLANT

SEEDS

How Do Carrots Grow?

Fun Fact: The longest carrot ever recorded was nearly 17 feet long.

CUT OUT THE PIECES AND PASTE THEM IN ORDER OF GROWTH

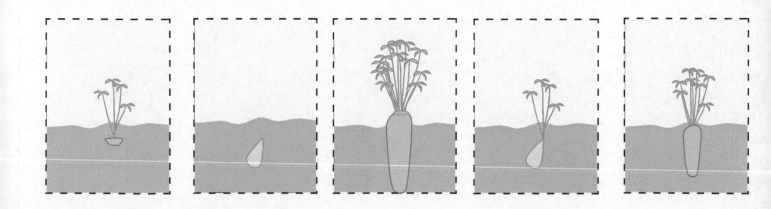

How Does Corn Grow?

Fun Fact: An average ear of corn has 800 kernels.

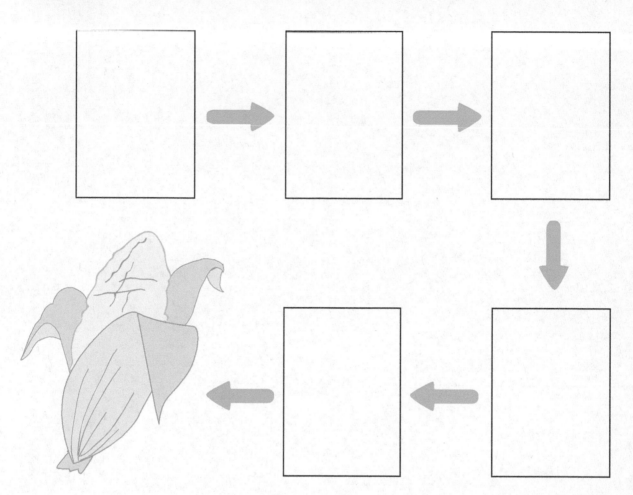

CUT OUT THE PIECES AND PASTE THEM IN ORDER OF GROWTH

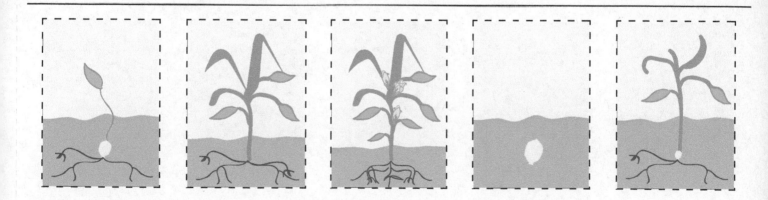

What is Photosynthesis

Study the picture below. Then use the diagram labels to complete the sentences at the bottom of the page.

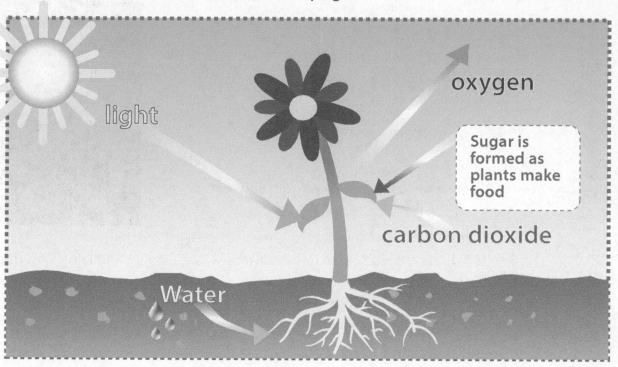

Photosynthesis is a process that plants use to breathe and to make food. They use the _____ from the sun, along with _____ in the soil and a gas called _____ _____ to make _____ , which feeds the plant. During this process, _____ is released into the air.

Celery Stick Science

All plants and animals need water to survive. But how does a plant drink its water? Find out what really happens when you sprinkle that water, with this fun experiment that shows how plants absorb water!

What You Need:
- Tall clear glass or jar
- Water
- Red food coloring
- Scissors
- Celery stalk with leaves
- Observation worksheet

What You Do:

1. Fill a tall, clear glass half-full with water.
2. Add a few drops of red food coloring and mix well.
3. Trim the bottom of a large stalk of celery, leaving the leaves on the stalk.
4. Place the celery stalk in the glass or jar. Leave overnight in order for the stalk to "drink" the water.
5. Use the observation sheet on the next page for this activity. Have your child draw a picture of the celery stalk "before" it drinks the red water and then write a sentence to describe what he sees.
6. The next morning, observe what has happened. Let your child tell you where he thinks the water has gone and what has happened to the celery. Ask him if he thinks the whole plant gets water for food, and help to guide him to see that yes, the whole plant did get the water for food since all parts of the plant have now turned red (from absorbing the red water that was in the cup the day before).
7. Have your child complete the "after" portion of the observation sheet. He can draw a picture of what happened and write a sentence to sum up his findings.

Celery Stick Science

Before

Draw a picture and describe what you see.

_____
_____

After

Draw a picture and describe what you see.

_____
_____

What's Happening?

The water has been absorbed into the celery stalk, tinting the stem and leaves red.

Conclusion

Write your thoughts and make a drawing about this experiment.

_____

Germinating Seeds

Seeds are baby plants. They have a thick, hard coat on them, just like a baby chick inside an egg. When conditions are right—good light, warm temperature, and moisture—the seedling comes out! In this activity, you'll germinate some seeds and watch as they grow into full size plants.

What You Need:

• Seeds of any kind
• Paper towel
• Stapler
• Plastic bag that zips
• Ruler
• Half cup of water
• Observation worksheet

What You Do:

1. Fold a paper towel and place it so that it fits just inside the plastic bag.

2. Use the ruler and measure 3 inches from the top of the bag. Staple a bunch of staples in a row across the bag. You should have a miniature pocket. Your seeds will sit here.

3. Pour the half cup of water into the bag so your seeds have something to drink.

4. Have your child put the seeds into the bag so that they rest between the plastic and the paper towel in the upper mini pocket you've created. Zip up the bag so that no air can get in or out. You've just made a mini green house!

5. Help your child tape your mini green house to a window for plenty of light.

6. Use the observation worksheet on the next page to track your seedlings' progress. Each day, check the green house together with your child and ask her what she thinks may be happening. Does she see anything beginning to sprout up?

7. After and few days-weeks you will see roots and seedlings beginning to form.

8. Carefully open your bag up and use a staple remover to remove the staples. The seedlings are fragile, so handle them with care! Once you've removed them, you can plant the sprouted seeds into a pot of soil. Make sure you cover just above the top of the seed, so that it is covered with about an inch of soil. You don't want to bury them! Nurture your new plant and see what it turns into.

Germinating Seeds

Use the spaces below to record the growth of the seeds you planted. Remember to write in the type of seed, the date you planted it, and the day you looked at it. Then draw a picture of any changes you see.

Type of Seed	Date Planted	Observation Date	Draw a Picture

Great job!

is an Education.com science superstar

WEATHER WATCHERS

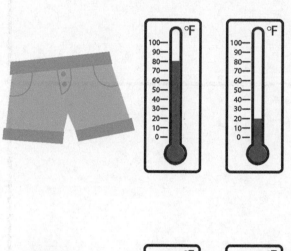

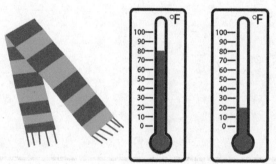

Weather Forecast

What was weather like yesterday? What is the weather like today? Can you predict what the weather will look like tomorrow? Use the boxes below to draw what the weather looks like outside.

Yesterday	Today	Tomorrow

Explain why the weather will be that way tomorrow.

_____

_____

_____

Weather Log: Choose a time of day and record the temperature in the bar graph below! Make sure to record the temperature at the same time, every day of the week. Use the space above the graph to draw what the weather looks like that day! Is the weather sunny, rainy, cloudy, or something else?

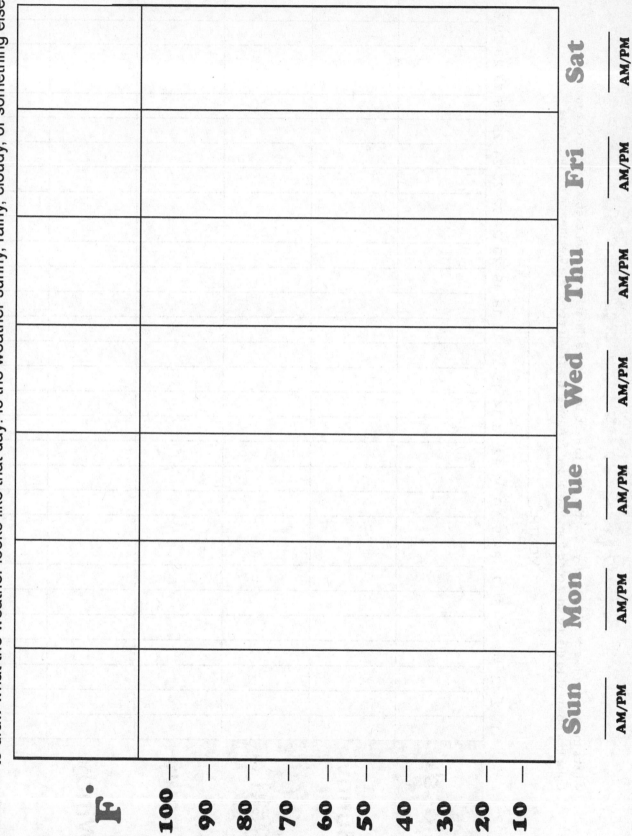

Graph the Weather!

What's the weather like out there today? Use the chart to keep track of the different weather events outside for a month. Color in a box next to the weather conditions you observe. Answer questions about the weather on the next page.

MONTH: _____

	1	2	3	4	5	6	7	8	9	10	11	12	13	14	15	16	17	18	19	20	21	22	23	24	25	26	27	28	29	30	31
Cloudy																															
Sunny																															
Rainy																															
Snowy																															
Windy																															
Foggy																															

Graph the Weather!

Now that you have watched and recorded the weather conditions, read your graph to answer some questions about this month's weather!

MONTH: _____

How many days were CLOUDY? _____

How many days were SUNNY? _____

How many days were RAINY? _____

How many days were SNOWY? _____

How many days were WINDY? _____

How many days were FOGGY? _____

Which weather condition occurred the most amount of days? _____

Which weather condition occurred the least amount of days? _____

Were there more SUNNY days or more RAINY days? _____

Were there more FOGGY days or more SNOWY days? _____

How many more CLOUDY days were there than SUNNY days? _____

How many more RAINY days were there than SUNNY days? _____

How many more CLOUDY days were there than WINDY days? _____

Which weather condition do you predict will occur the most days next month? _____

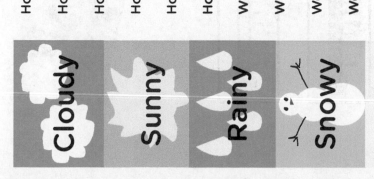

Hot or Cold?

What should you wear? Circle the thermometer that goes with each item of clothing.

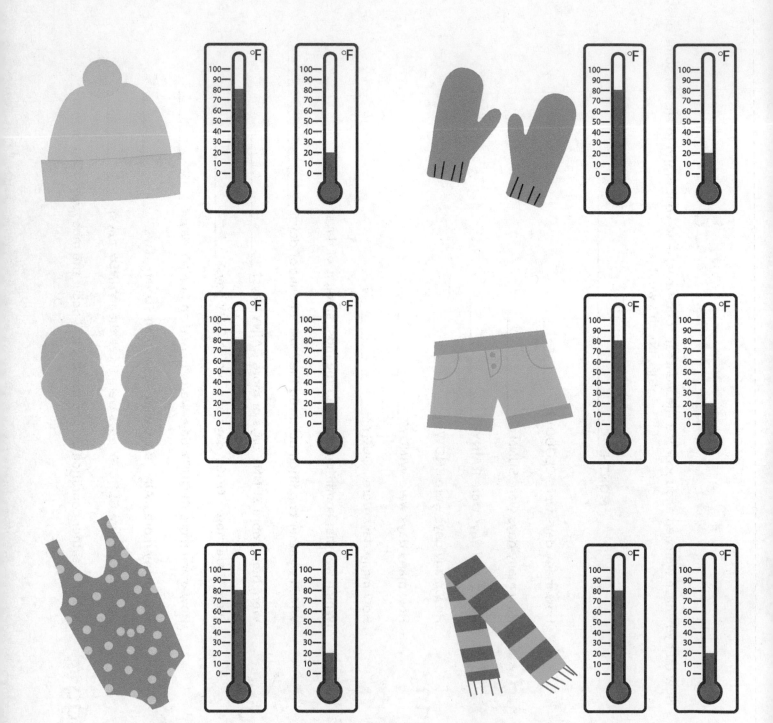

What's the Temperature?

Look at the thermometers and write down the correct temperature.

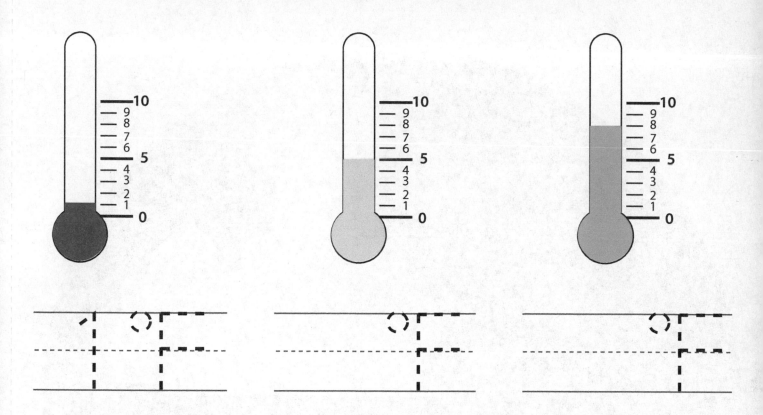

Now color in the thermometer to match the temperature written.

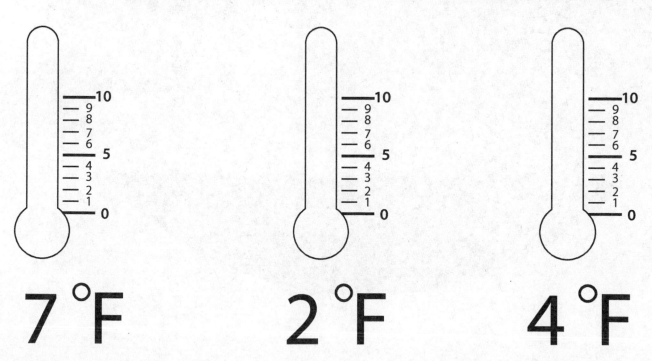

7°F   2°F   4°F

Water Cycle Diagram

Water Cycle Terms

Directions:

Cut out the labels and glue them where they belong on the Weather Cycle diagram!

Sun

Cloud

Rain

Ocean

Evaporation

Condensation

Precipitation

Complete the
Water Cycle

This water cycle diagram needs some more color!
Read the description of each part of the cycle, then draw a picture of the missing steps.

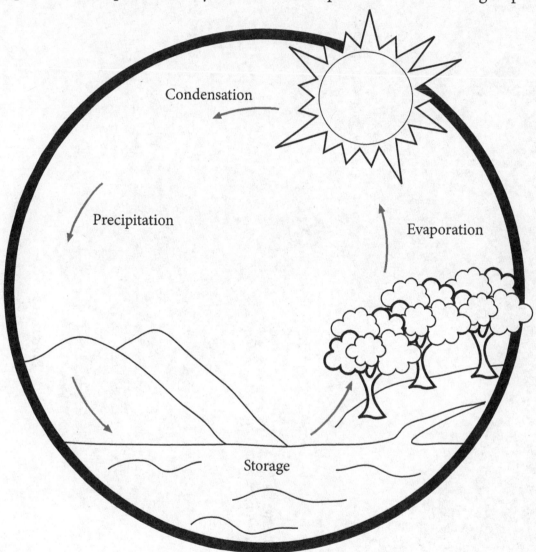

Evaporation:

The sun heats the ocean water and turns some of it into vapor.

Condensation:

The vapor gathers and turns into clouds.

Precipitation:

Clouds move around in the sky and fall back to earth as fog, rain, or snow.

Storage:

The precipitation is absorbed by the ground or bodies of water.

Types of Clouds

Cirrostratus
high-altitude, thin, wispy sheet

Cirrus
high-altitude, feathery, thin, curly

Stratus
low-altitude, thin, wispy, grey

Cirrocumulus
high-altitude, small, patchy, puffy

Nimbus
low-altitude, dark, large, dense

Cumulus
low-altitude, fluffy

Snow Facts

Snow is made when the air in the sky is so cold that it freezes the water droplets in the clouds. Then the water droplets become frozen ice crystals.

As temperatures reach freezing, more and more water will collect on the ice crystal. When it gets too heavy, it falls!

Water comes in three states: solid, liquid, and gas. Snow is water in a solid form, rain is water in liquid form, and clouds are water in gas form!

Each ice crystal (or snowflake) has a different shape, depending on the air temperature and how much water vapor there is.

Each snowflake has a shape entirely its own! Can you draw some unique snowflakes in the box below?

Wind Facts

Wind is *moving air*!

It happens because the sun heats up the earth's surface unevenly—high mountains and low valleys absorb the sun's energy differently. The same thing happens in the air. Some parts of the air are colder, and some are warmer.

Warm air weighs less than cold air, so it rises up, and cold air replaces it. Wind happens when the cold and warm air move around in the sky.

Wind currents have a role in shaping and moving clouds in the sky! Can you use the Types of Clouds worksheet (p. 108) to identify these clouds?

Wind at Work

Wind is moving air. We can't see wind, but we can see it move things. Sometimes we can hear it and even feel it!

What can wind do? Fill in the blanks from your own experience!

Wind can blow a _____.

Wind can fly a _____.

Wind can shake a _____.

Wind can make a _____ go faster.

I can hear the wind when _____.

I can feel the wind when _____.

Draw a picture of a windy day. Show the wind at work!

Weathervane

A weathervane is one of the most useful tools for forecasting, because certain winds bring certain weather patterns.

If the wind is blowing from the south, the wind is usually warm. If the wind is blowing from the north, the wind is usually cooler.

Weathervanes are usually found on the tops of buildings so they can catch an open breeze. Can you think of some good places to put a weather vane?

Weathervanes can only measure wind direction a few yards off the ground. Large, helium-filled weather balloons (like this one) are used to measure winds high above the earth's surface.

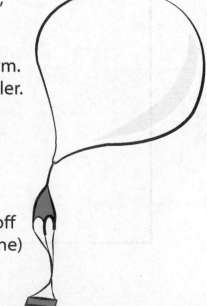

Windsock Project

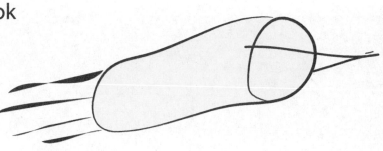

Supplies:
Pages 113 and 115 of this book
String
Glue or tape
Hole punch
Crayons
Scissors

Directions:
First, cut out these colorful strips! Then, follow the rest of the directions on page 115.

Cut out the strips along the black lines!

How to make a windsock:

1. Flip this page over and decorate the back side of it however you like. *Note: The top edge of this picture (the edge with the red dots) will be the bottom of the windsock.*

2. Cut out the paper strips on page 1.

3. Glue or tape the paper strips onto the red dots on the edge of this page.

4. Once the glue dries, roll your picture hamburger-style until the ends meet. (The strips should be on the inside, your picture on the outside.) Glue, staple, or tape your windsock in the shape of a cylinder.

5. Punch two holes on opposite sides at the top of your wind sock. Thread the string through both holes, pull the ends together, and tie a knot at the top.

6. Hold the wind sock by the knot and take it outside to see which way the wind is blowing!

Make a Weathervane

Wondering which way the wind blows? Is there a storm brewing? Your child can learn more about earth science as well as meteorology through learning how to make a weathervane! All that's needed are materials you probably have in the pantry, and items that can be recycled—perfect for an Earth happy project!

What You Need:

- Old business card
- Straw
- Ruler
- Scissors
- Clear tape
- Pencil
- Stickpin
- 1 liter plastic bottle
- Sand
- Compass
- Black permanent marker

What You Do:

1. Start by researching with your child what a weathervane is and what purpose it serves by visiting your local library or looking online. Many people have decorative weathervanes on their roofs.

2. Help your child gather the materials needed to create his own weathervane. Offer assistance cutting the liter bottle in half if necessary.

3. Now he can cut a triangle out of the business card to create the front and back ends of the weathervane. He can also trim the straw so it is 6 inches long. If the straw has a flexible end, make sure it's the end that is cut.

4. Invite your child to carefully cut slits into both ends of the straw, about half an inch deep horizontally, and slide the cut card onto each end. He can secure each of the ends with a small piece of clear tape.

5. Offer your child the pencil and stick pin and encourage him to use the ruler to find the middle of the straw. Now he can position the pencil under the straw and secure the two together with the stickpin creating to top of his weathervane!

6. To create the weathervane base, invite your child to fill the cut bottom of the plastic bottle with some sand, and firmly stick the pencil weathervane into the center of the sand.

7. Now your child can place his weathervane in a windy spot and observe how it moves with the wind. Invite your child to guess which direction the wind's blowing, and then use a compass to check his guesses. He can even use a permanent marker to write the directions on the side of the plastic bottle if he wants!

Weather Terminology Word Search

A	Y	R	A	I	N	Y	W	H	Z	B	P	A	M	W
P	D	D	J	L	J	Q	A	U	T	A	U	I	R	D
M	N	P	M	C	N	Y	R	H	R	C	L	M	O	P
I	I	N	X	J	S	O	M	T	Y	D	O	Q	B	R
Y	W	S	G	X	D	W	L	U	L	G	D	L	E	E
K	B	H	K	L	D	Y	Q	V	X	T	G	D	D	Q
W	W	X	F	T	C	S	K	Z	V	O	U	O	J	K
Z	K	C	U	L	G	N	I	Z	E	E	R	F	F	F
R	T	Z	O	T	O	H	T	D	J	D	G	W	S	T
S	X	U	J	Q	W	G	F	P	S	V	J	X	P	Y
U	D	A	N	D	F	W	B	U	V	L	H	L	N	D
Y	B	Z	E	U	R	R	R	A	H	Z	G	N	Q	K
C	X	Z	S	I	W	I	H	F	X	K	U	P	Q	S
I	J	G	L	M	Z	I	T	C	S	S	P	V	Q	Z
J	W	R	V	F	O	B	P	N	E	C	C	J	O	F

Word Bank:

foggy	cloudy	cold	freezing
sunny	windy	warm	mild
rainy	partly cloudy	hot	

Great job!

is an Education.com science superstar

ANSWERS

Hunting For Animal Homes

Animals need shelter in order to survive, and there are many different types of animal homes! Can you find these different shelters in the word puzzle below?

HINT: *Make sure you look backwards and diagonally.*

Word Bank:

house	underground	tunnel	tree	pond	ocean	forest
cave	nest	hive	den	burrow	web	barn
kennel	stable	coop	sty			

```
H  L  E  N  P  X  W  P  O  N  D  B  K  E  Z
F  P  S  A  L  Z  J  N  U  N  X  Z  S  E  W
Y  Q  I  E  B  Q  Y  Q  U  N  B  N  S  T  Y
H  U  R  C  C  B  B  O  H  F  Q  E  G  N  H
H  Y  Y  O  E  X  R  C  C  Q  M  D  O  U  E
H  Z  X  W  Q  G  T  P  A  O  P  M  P  B  U
B  T  F  R  R  N  G  N  Q  V  I  W  S  N  D
S  I  T  E  H  G  B  W  E  T  E  J  L  E  K
I  L  D  I  E  L  B  A  T  S  W  H  K  S  H
A  N  V  I  F  A  U  H  T  D  U  E  R  T  B
U  E  I  X  Z  O  R  R  L  H  N  O  G  B  W
T  U  N  N  E  L  R  E  X  N  P  E  H  Z  I
J  E  A  W  Z  V  O  E  E  X  E  O  E  Q  J
N  R  A  B  A  S  W  L  S  R  N  N  O  L  F
Y  S  V  N  X  C  T  P  T  T  H  Q  M  C  R
```

page 7

Weather Terminology
Word Search

```
A Y R A I N Y W H Z B P A M W
P D D J L J Q A U T A U I R D
M N P M C N Y R H R C L M O P
I I N X J S O M T Y D O Q B R
Y W S G X D W L U L G D L E E
K B H K L D Y Q V X T G D D Q
W W X F T C S K Z V O U O J K
Z K C U L G N I Z E E R F F F
R T Z O T O H T D J D G W S T
S Y U J Q W G F P S V J X P Y
U D A N D F W B U V L H L N D
Y B Z E U R R R A H Z G N Q K
C X Z S I W I H F X K U P Q S
I J G L M Z I T C S S P V Q Z
J W R V F O B P N E C C J O F
```

Word Bank:

foggy	cloudy	cold	freezing
sunny	windy	warm	mild
rainy	partly cloudy	hot	